Tasting the Sounds

Finn Harris

Presentation by *BookLeaf Publishing*

Web: www.bookleafpub.com

E-mail: info@bookleafpub.com

ISBN: 9789357441827

First edition 2023

*This book is dedicated to the natural world.
It can teach priceless life lessons, we just
need to pay close attention to see them.*

To One's Young Self

Take a breath my boy
The deep end is not so deep
Just know you will float

Who's Next?

Never fear the promised end
For there is a promised beginning
To another begin, not you
You have had your turn to see the view
Move aside and take a bow
It is out of your hands now
You have tasted the water and felt the air
You have been caught in snares and learned to
share
Lessons overlooked in the moment
Reflecting back they were potent
Now keep in mind all you have been
Hands off the wheel
This moment will be surreal

Abyss to Bliss

Immense emotions run
Learning without question
Nonstop until my heart is done
Craving love an obsession

Eyes met and instantly fell
Seeming forever falling
Within my thoughts you dwell
The promised end I am stalling

Keep my eyes on you
Never will I need to blink
Colors of love a beautiful hue
Meer seconds away and I sink

Sink deep into the abyss
My one savior a kiss
Now we exist in utter bliss

Recollections of Relatable Experiences

Nothing like the feeling of ocean water on the lips.
How simple it may seem in the moment, unpleasant even.
Yet, how I would like nothing more.
Sand dunes block the sound, the wind, and an array of sensations.
Sensations well muted until cresting the sand hill, all coming to life at once.
Remember that feeling of the hot board walk?
I should've waited to take my shoes off until I got to the sand.
Speaking of sand and feet, that's the feeling everyone remembers, it is truly one of a kind.

Oh, then there are the mountains.
So many surfaces to walk and rest upon.
Compacted soil, rocks, and sticks from a thousand footsteps.
A collection of rocks pushed against the forest, built by water.
One large stone, cold at first touch, then warmed by my resting body.

Resting in place is nice, until I move and hit a
cold stone surrounding my profile, waking me
from my half sleeping half coherent nap.
Soft grass, untouched by the weight of man.
As well as grass in the path, but unlike the soil,
it rebounds following each footstep.
All seasons are true here.
One day from each and you've lived an entire
year.
Biting temperatures, frozen riverbanks, clean
wind, and intense silence.
Retreating cold moves north, colorful plant life
occupies my eyes.
Soaring temperatures make a dip in the frigid
river a necessity to survive.
Lastly, before the cycle begins again, the
animals and trees alike enjoying life's bounty go
through the mandatory changes for survival.

Of course, these are very few of my many
memories worth mentioning.
For now, I am an old version of myself and here
with my thoughts.
Recollections, really.
All the things I remember are relatable for most,
yet they are my own version.
The sensations are still very much alive.
In my mind they thrive.

Time for What We Are

There is time for sadness
Time for happiness
For madness
Kindness

There is time to forgive
Time to live
Give

There is no illusion
Remember we are human
We are trying
Dying
Crying
Flying

Individuals we may be
Going and doing as we please
We must cohere
Otherwise the future is most unclear

Unexpected Turn of Events

It is the very reason I want to go
All the signs clearly show it should not be so
I feel so good and confident
What could go wrong?
Grab my keys
Hop in my car
Blast the tunes
Hoping to drive fast and far
Where am I? This does not feel right.
Welcome to the afterlife kid
So, remember that vodka you had the other
night?

Friday Fish Fry for Friends

Finn fished for Friday's fish fry for friends,
Furthermore, frying fish for forty four friends
for Friday felt frightening for Finn.

At Best, Comfort Deepens
Even Further

Above all, accept absolute abstract ability.
Before bailing, be better because beauty beats
buffoonery.
Continually calling caddies cannot curate
creativity.
Demanding demons dancing darkens dawns
dewy delight.
Earth's edges ease eager eyes, enlighten even.
Freedom finds fortitude, for fortitude fears
futility.

False Church

Your brothers and sister have twisted my words
In such a way that gets them their say
Time and time again I try to show them
all-powerful is a bit much
Yes, I care for those little boys and girls.
If I could stop the hunger and pain, I would
The ones altering my wants and desires fear me,
rightfully so
They have turned sour and will be devoured

Freedom Within

Drifting and floating with the tide
Gripping reality with all my might
Contemplating simply letting go
If I held, if I release, what will become of me?
Is there a place?
A place of peace between the two extremes to reside?
Ah, I found such a spot
All I had to do was close my eyes
For this kind of find is in our mind

See, Taste, and Smell the World

To the places I have been
The places I will go
Far away from home
People I will know

Scents I will smell
Flavors I will taste
For the night I will dwell
For a time, I am displaced

Tis a good thing I say
There are things to see
No matter how far I sway

What am I?

Continually flowing without concern
Effortlessly finding the easy path
Simple life
One goal
One mind
Sometimes a bit taken aside
Sometimes a bit left behind
There is no end to this journey
Only different times
Different places
Seen countless faces in all the phases
No escaping this physical fate
Back and forth from filthy to healthy
Nevertheless
Plugging away to fulfill the ultimate purpose
Provide life no matter the plight

People are Feeble

Seals live on blocks of ice
Birds can soar above
Fish can dwell deep beneath
Cats can see in the dark and climb trees
Humans can do all those things too
But they need machines because they are so
weak

Ode to Rock Climbing

Cheers for the grips
Cheers for the grabs
You keep me running back
Even while carrying a big pad, a fucking heavy
one at that
So stoked to be out and see what there is to clean
then climb
The sport is more than sport
You thought I was going to say it's a lifestyle,
huh
It's more like a cokehead getting a snort
 Just a feen looking for the next fix
Not just climbing, it's a mix
A mix of nature and the climbing itself
You see, I just want to be outside
I want to see new places and faces
I challenge myself at different paces
Climbing allows me to express myself via
climbing a rock
How silly is that?
Just as silly as everything else humans do, and
that's a fact
Surprising enough, climbing is meaningful in its
own right
Thank you rock climbing

Your appeal is binding
I found you with perfect timing

Cease to Overthink

Sipping wine on a fine crisp night
Chipping away the way a chisel may
Gripping until the chill subsides

Put my feet upon the path and they will walk
For the path is arduous and tortuous
Blind the eyes from pain and the brain will feel
no more

Profound feelings may arise as the skies
Feelings dealing with despise among our demise
Just keep sipping wine and all will shine

To Win Always is Impossible

Stay humble my boy
Run slowly my boy
Remain patient through it all
Sometimes take the fall

Home Away from Home

There is always somewhere you yearn to return
Not where you live and sleep,
But a place to keep
Keep close to your heart
It is always bittersweet to depart
You know you will be back

Letter of Admittance

Bricks are like the pieces of my life
As well as the aspects of your wife
They keep me firm yet relaxed
Thank you for telling her to stay waxed
Hope this poem doesn't cause any strife

www.ingramcontent.com/pod-product-compliance
Lightning Source LLC
LaVergne TN
LVHW050308200726

843509LV00015B/3217